Warfare

Peter Chrisp

WAYLAND

Titles in the series:

Art and Architecture

Daily Life

Death and Disease

Education

Monarchs

Warfare

Published in 2014 by Hodder Wayland
An imprint of Hodder Children's Books
First published in 2004 by Hodder Wayland
Text copyright © 2014 Hodder Wayland
Volume copyright © 2014 Hodder Wayland

Design: Peta Morey
Commissioning Editor: Jane Tyler
Editor: Liz Gogerly
Picture Researcher: Glass Onion Pictures
Consultant: Malcolm Barber
Map artwork: Encompass

We are grateful to the following for permission to reproduce photographs:
Art Archive 5 (top), 7, 9, 10, 11, 12, 15, 16, 21, 22, 23, 27, 28, 31, 33, 35, 36, 38, 39, 41(bottom); Bridgeman/ Nationalmuseet, Copenhagen, Denmark 5 (bottom)/ Kunstindustrimuseet, Oslo, Norway 8/ Private Collection 14, 37, 40/ Bibliotheque des Arts Decoratifs, Paris, France 18/ Centre Historique des Archives Nationales, Paris, France 19/ Bibliotheque Nationale, Paris France 20/ Collection of the Earl of Leicester, Holkam Hall, Norfolk, England 30/ Lambeth Palace Library, London, England 32/ Basilique Saint-Denis, Paris, France 34/ National Museum, Stockholm, Sweden 44; British Armoury 41 (top and bottom), 43, 45 (top); British Library (*title*), 6; British Museum 13; Martyn Chillmaid 29; Corbis 42; Mary Evans 26; Topham Picturepoint 24, 25 (top and bottom)

Cover picture: Shutterstock/Titania; Wolfgang Zwanzger; Mark William Penny; Neiron Photo (clockwise)

Printed in China

Warfare: – (Medieval realms)
1. Military art and science – Europe – History – Medieval,
2. 500-1500 2. Military history, Medieval 3. Europe – History, Military
I. Title
II. 355'.004'0902

ISBN 978 0 7502 8472 1

Hodder Children's Books
A division of Hodder Headline Limited
338 Euston Road, London NW1 3BH

*Please note: dates after names of monarchs refer to dates of reign unless otherwise stated. Words in **bold** can be found in the glossary on page 47.*

Contents

Warrior Nobles

IN THE EARLY eleventh century, most of Europe was ruled by **nobles** whose main purpose in life was warfare. They had their own set of values, which prized bravery and loyalty to one's lord above everything else. In return for this loyalty, lords were expected to give protection and wealth to their military followers. **Warrior** nobles looked down on anybody who had to work for a living.

Raiding Warfare

War was a profitable business, which could bring wealth and power. Its most common form was the raid, the sudden unexpected attack by land or sea. Raiders burned towns, villages and farms, and seized any wealth that they could find.

Arms and Armour

Eleventh-century warriors wore knee-length coats of iron mail and conical helmets with nose guards. In most of Europe, they fought on horseback, carrying long kite-shaped shields, **lances** and swords. In the northern lands of England and Scandinavia, warriors rode to battle but fought on foot. The deadliest northern weapon was the **battleaxe**.

In the year 1030, Europe included several kingdoms, such as France and England, and two empires, the German and the Byzantine, which also ruled parts of the Middle East. To the south lay Muslim lands, including much of Spain.

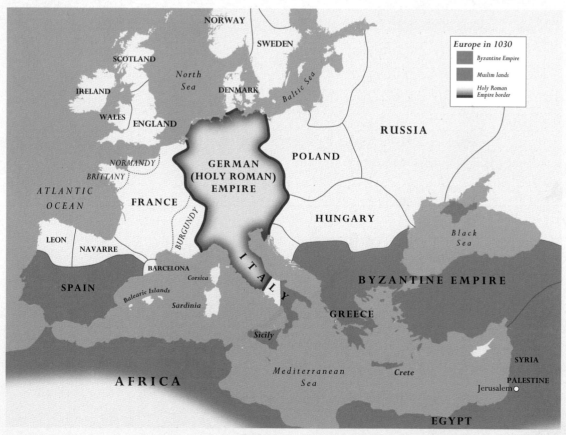

Europe in 1030
- Byzantine Empire
- Muslim lands
- Holy Roman Empire border

NORWAY
SWEDEN
SCOTLAND
North Sea
IRELAND
DENMARK
Baltic Sea
WALES
ENGLAND
RUSSIA
NORMANDY
POLAND
BRITTANY
GERMAN (HOLY ROMAN) EMPIRE
ATLANTIC OCEAN
FRANCE
HUNGARY
BURGUNDY
Black Sea
LEON
NAVARRE
BARCELONA
Corsica
ITALY
BYZANTINE EMPIRE
SPAIN
Balearic Islands
Sardinia
GREECE
Sicily
Mediterranean Sea
Crete
Cyprus
SYRIA
AFRICA
PALESTINE
Jerusalem
EGYPT

From the year 1002, King Svein Forkbeard of Denmark (987–1014) made annual raids across the North Sea to England, demanding vast sums of silver to leave the English in peace. Svein used this wealth to attract even more warriors. By 1013 he had such a strong army that he was able to seize the English crown.

Meanwhile, Spain, mostly ruled by Muslims, was regularly raided by Christian knights from the north. Like the Danes attacking England, the knights asked for '**protection money**' from their victims, who were rich but had few fighting men. In his memoirs, Abd Allah, the Muslim ruler of Granada, wrote, 'I knew that paying 10,000 a year for protection was better than the devastation of the land.'

Harald Hardrada

Harald Hardrada ('Hard Ruler') was the half-brother of the Norwegian king, Olaf the Good (1015–1030). In 1030, when Olaf was killed in battle, the fifteen-year-old Harald fled south to Constantinople, capital of the **Byzantine Empire**. He became a **mercenary** in the service of the emperor. After fifteen years raiding in the Mediterranean, Harald had collected so much gold that he was able to return home and use his wealth to make himself king of Norway.

To a man like Harald, war brought fame and glory, which was just as important as money and power. The king had his own court poets, called *skalds*, who praised his skill at killing his enemies.

This Italian manuscript of the 1020s shows warriors wearing knee-length mail coats as they gallop into battle.

One of Harald Hardrada's court poets, called Thjodolf, described the warrior's campaigns in the Mediterranean:

'**All men know that Harald
Fought eighteen savage battles;
Wherever the warrior went
All hope of peace was shattered.
The grey eagle's talons [claws]
You reddened with blood, great king;
On all your expeditions
    The hungry wolves were feasted.**'

A poem of *circa* 1050 quoted in *King Harald's Saga, circa* 1235.

Scandinavian battleaxes, sometimes richly decorated, were highly prized possessions, and often given their own names, such as 'leg-biter'.

War and the Church

HARALD HARDRADA (1045–1066) was a ruthless killer.
Yet he was also a Christian and a firm supporter of the Church.
While fighting for the emperor of the **Byzantine Empire**, he
went on a **pilgrimage**, or holy journey, to the tomb of Jesus
Christ in Jerusalem and gave treasures to the church there.
Back in Norway, he built a fine church to hold the bones of
his half-brother, Olaf, who had been declared a saint.

Churchmen, like the monk who painted this picture, hoped that knights would be firm Christians. This praying knight is covered in crosses.

Peace of God

In the early eleventh century, an anti-war movement, called the 'Peace of God', was started by churchmen in southern France. They said that, if fighting could not be avoided, it should be limited to particular days. There should be no fighting from Thursday until Sunday, days all linked in some way with Jesus Christ. Thursday, for example, was the day on which he was believed to have risen to heaven. Certain groups, such as the poor, should be recognized as **'non-combatants'**, people whom it was unlawful to harm. Although it attracted wide support, the movement was unable to change the behaviour of the warlike French nobles.

A praying knight receives a cross from a hermit, a type of Christian holy man, before setting off on a crusade (see page 14).

When Harald was young, most Norwegians still worshipped the old Viking gods, Thor and Odin. For Harald, the great attraction of Christianity lay in the prestige it gave to kingship. The Church taught that royal power came from God, and so a king was set above his subjects. Harald gained even greater prestige by having a saint for a half-brother.

'You Shall Not Kill'

Churchmen had mixed feelings about men like Harald. They were glad that they had strong Christian rulers to protect them from attack. Yet the Bible said, 'You shall not kill.' Killing was a sin, an act which angered God, and those who shed blood would suffer terrible punishments after death.

The only way to avoid punishment was to perform a **penance**, an action making amends to God. Penances included saying prayers, fasting (going without food), or going on a pilgrimage. After battles, whole armies were sometimes ordered to fast as penance for the blood on their hands.

A Just War?

Medieval churchmen struggled with the problem of whether it was possible to wage a just war, a question which still troubles us today. They decided that warfare could only be just if it obeyed three conditions. The war had to be declared by a proper authority, such as a king or the pope. It had to be fought for a just cause, such as resisting evil. Most difficult of all, the soldiers fighting had to have right intentions. If they felt the desire to hurt for gain, they would not be fighting a just war. By such standards, few, if any, medieval wars could be called just.

A French monk described the beginning of the 'Peace of God' movement:

'It was decreed that in fixed places the bishops and lords should summon councils for re-establishing peace ... When the people heard this, the great, those of middle rank, and the poor, all came rejoicing ... Such enthusiasm was created that ... all cried out with one voice to God, their hands stretched out: "Peace! Peace! Peace!"'

Five Books of Histories, Ralph Glaber, *circa* 1040.

The Normans

IN THE ELEVENTH CENTURY, the most successful **warriors** in Europe were the Normans, the people of Normandy, on the north coast of France. They were called Normans, or 'north men', because they had originally been Viking raiders from Denmark and Norway. After raiding northern France, they had settled there in the early tenth century. They married French wives, became Christians and learned to speak French. From 1035, the ruler of Normandy was Duke William, later called William the Conqueror.

England

A short distance across the sea to the north lay the rich kingdom of England. In the 1060s, the land was ruled by King Edward the Confessor (1042–1066), an old man with no son to succeed him. According to Norman accounts, Edward, whose mother was Norman, promised the throne to William, whom he loved like a son. In 1064, Edward sent his most powerful **noble**, Earl Harold Godwinson, to visit William in Normandy. Harold was said to have sworn an oath on the bones of a saint, either to help William become king, or to be his **vassal**.

Despite this oath, when Edward died on 5 January 1066 it was Harold, not William, who was made king. The Witan, the council of leading nobles and churchmen, offered the throne to Harold, who was crowned on the day after Edward's death.

Norman barons

The chief nobles of Normandy, known as barons, were said to 'hold' their lands from the duke, rather than own them. For this privilege, they had to swear an oath of **fealty** (loyalty). They became the duke's vassals (loyal servants). In wartime, they fought for the duke and provided him with knights and footsoldiers.

This Norwegian tapestry shows a typical Norman or Scandinavian warrior.

In this scene from the Bayeux Tapestry William's fleet crosses the sea to England. The famous tapestry shows the invasion from the Norman point of view.

Preparing for War

As soon as he learned that Harold was king, William decided to invade England and seize the crown. Arguing that Harold had broken a holy oath, he won the backing of the Pope, the head of the Church in western Europe. William could now claim to be fighting for a just and holy cause. He would ride to battle with a bag around his neck, holding the saint's bones on which Harold had sworn his oath.

It took William seven months to prepare for the invasion. He built a fleet of around 700 ships, and assembled an army of 7,000 men, including 2,000–3,000 mounted knights. Alongside the Normans, there were knights from many other parts of France. They joined the army as volunteers, attracted by the promise of sharing in the wealth of England.

English and Norman accounts of how Harold became king are very different:

'Yet the wise king [Edward] entrusted his kingdom to a man of high rank, to Harold himself, the noble earl, who ever faithfully obeyed his noble lord in words and deeds.'

The Anglo-Saxon Chronicle, a collection of year-by-year histories of England written by English monks between the ninth and the twelfth centuries.

'This unfeeling Englishman (Harold) ... breaking his oath, and with a few evil followers, seized the throne of the best of kings on the very day of his funeral.'

The Deeds of William, William of Poitiers, *circa* 1074.

9

1066: The Year of Three Battles

WHILE WILLIAM was preparing his invasion, Harold in England was also raising troops, which he stationed along the south coast. He also gathered a war fleet of around 700 ships, which he based off the Isle of Wight, waiting for the Normans.

For six weeks, a north wind prevented William's fleet from sailing. This was a difficult period for both leaders, who faced the problem of feeding their armies. By 8 September, the men of the English fleet had run out of supplies, and Harold was forced to send them home.

Norwegian Invasion

After dismissing his fleet, Harold heard dreadful news. There was another claimant to the English crown, Harald Hardrada (1045–1066), the bloodthirsty king of Norway. In September, Hardrada invaded the north of England with 300 ships. He sailed upriver to York, where, on 20 September, he defeated the

Fyrdmen and Housecarls

The English army, called the fyrd, was made up of **militiamen**. In wartime, free men might be called up to serve for a limited period, usually two months, in the fyrd. Harold also had a small force of around 1,000 full-time **warriors**, called **housecarls**. English housecarls, armed with huge **battleaxes**, were probably the toughest footsoldiers in all of Europe.

In this scene from the Bayeux Tapestry, the English stand in a tight shield-wall, fighting off attacks by the Norman cavalry at Hastings.

This thirteenth-century picture falsely shows William personally killing Harold at the Battle of Hastings.

northern English army in battle.

Leaving the south undefended, Harold of England rushed north with his housecarls to meet this new threat. On 25 September, he made a surprise attack on the Norwegian camp at Stamford Bridge outside York. In the bloody battle that followed, Harald Hardrada was killed along with most of his army. So many Norwegians were killed that just twenty-four ships were enough to take the survivors home.

Hastings

On 27 September, while Harold was still in the north, the wind at last changed direction, allowing William to cross the Channel. He landed unopposed, and set up a camp near Hastings in Sussex. At this news, Harold hastily rode south again. After five days in London, raising fresh troops, he marched towards Hastings to meet William.

On 14 October, at daybreak, Harold and his army took up a position on a high broad ridge. Standing shoulder to shoulder in a line called a 'shield wall', the English waited to meet the Norman attack. First William sent **archers** and footsoldiers against the English, but they could make no impression on the shield wall. Then waves of knights charged uphill, only to be driven back by the housecarls, swinging their great battleaxes.

The turning point came when the knights attacking the hill pretended to retreat. At this, many English broke ranks and came rushing down the hill, only for the knights to wheel round and cut them down. Under repeated attacks, the remaining shield wall began to break up. At last a group of Norman knights broke through and killed the English king.

An English monk from Worcester, England, described Harold's last stand:

'Until dusk, he bravely withstood the enemy, and fought so valiantly and stubbornly in his own defence that the enemy's forces could hardly make any headway. At last, after great slaughter on both sides, about twilight, the king, alas, fell.'

Chronicon ex Chronicis.

11

Castles

THE NORMANS had beaten the English in battle, yet they were still a small minority in a hostile land. In order to rule in safety, William (1066–1087) had to build castles throughout his kingdom. These were common on the continent but almost unknown in England before 1066.

Motte and Bailey

In forty towns, the English were forced to pull down their own houses to make space for castles. They also had to clear an area surrounding each castle, to prevent enemies getting close without being seen. The next task was to pile up a huge earth mound, called a **motte**. On top of this, a tall square tower, called a keep, was built.

Beside the motte, there was a **bailey**, or yard, enclosed by a high wall. The bailey was crammed with buildings, including

Castles and Warfare

The spread of castles changed the way that wars were fought. **Sieges** became much more common than battles. **Pitched battles**, like the Battle of Hastings, would be comparatively rare throughout the Middle Ages, because of the high risks involved. The costs of defeat could be terrible, as the deaths of the kings of England and Norway in the battles of 1066 show. It was often safer to avoid battle, and take refuge in a castle.

The Norman castle at Rochester, built in timber at a time of the conquest, was rebuilt in stone in 1087–1089. This was one of the first English stone castles.

Square towers were eventually replaced by stronger round ones, like the tower being built in this picture.

granaries, stables, workshops, a chapel and a hall for feasts. These first English castles were built in a hurry, using wood. In time, they were all rebuilt in stone.

Apart from its practical functions, the purpose of the castle was to overawe the people. Dominating each town, the castle reminded the English that the Normans were now in charge.

Bases for Rebellion

Castles gave **nobles** their own strongholds, which could be used as bases for rebellion against an unpopular or weak king. England had a strong central government before 1066, partly because the leading nobles, lacking such strongholds, found it much harder to rebel. At the same time France, where castles were widespread, had weak kings and powerful nobles.

In 1137, there was a widespread rebellion against the fourth Norman king, Stephen (1135–1154). According to an English monk, 'Every great man built him castles and held them against the king.' Stephen lost control of his kingdom, and his nineteen-year reign is described by historians as a time of **anarchy**.

A monk described the behaviour of the Norman barons who rebelled against King Stephen in 1137:

'They filled the whole land with these castles ... and when the castles were built, they filled them with devils and wicked men. By night and day they seized those whom they believed to have any wealth ... and tortured them with unspeakable tortures ... They levied a tax, known as 'tenserie' [protection money] upon the villages. When the wretched people had no more to give, they plundered and burned all the villages.'

The Anglo-Saxon Chronicle.

Holy War

ON 27 NOVEMBER 1095, Pope Urban II held a great meeting in a field outside the town of Clermont in France. He made a speech to a big crowd of **nobles** and churchmen, in which he called on the knights of Europe to stop fighting each other. Instead, they should fight a **crusade**, or Christian holy war, against the Muslims who ruled the Middle East.

The pope said that Muslims were the 'enemies of God', so it was no sin to kill them. Christians who killed Muslims did not need to perform a **penance** to make amends to God. The pope went further, and said that killing God's enemies was itself an act of penance, like a **pilgrimage**. So by fighting the crusade, the knights would be wiping out their sins. The listening knights took this to mean that if they died in battle, they would be rewarded in heaven. However, victory was certain, for the crusaders would have God on their side. The crowd listened to the pope's words with growing excitement, and began to shout out 'God wills it!' This became the battle cry of the First Crusade.

In this nineteenth-century engraving, Pope Urban proclaims the crusade to a vast crowd of knights who have gathered at Clermont, France.

According to a witness who was at Clermont, this is how the pope described Jerusalem, the goal of the crusade, in his speech:

'Our saviour [Jesus Christ] lit up this land by His coming ... This royal city, set in the centre of the world, is now held captive by His enemies, enslaved by those who do not know God. Therefore she demands to be set free, and calls upon you ceaselessly to come to her aid.'

The Expedition to Jerusalem, Robert the Monk, 1106.

Crusaders

The pope's message was intended only for the knights of Europe. Yet his idea of a holy war was so powerful that ordinary people wanted to play a part. In northern France and Germany, popular preachers spread the word. Peasants left their fields before the harvest and townspeople left their homes, joining a movement called the 'People's Crusade'. Over the next six years, as many as 130,000 Europeans set off for the east. Only a tenth of them were knights.

The Battle of Muret, fought in 1213 by French crusaders against fellow Frenchmen, who had been called 'heretics' by the Church.

The official army of the Crusade comprised knights from much of western Europe. There were Normans, commanded by Duke Robert of Normandy, son of William the Conqueror. Knights from Southern Italy were led by another Norman, Bohemond of Taranto. French knights served under Godfrey of Bouillon and Raymond of Toulouse. Small groups of Germans and Spaniards also took part. In late 1096, they set off on their long journey to Jersualem.

Crusading in Europe

Crusading was later used by the Church against its enemies in Europe. In the north-east lands by the Baltic, there were crusades against pagans – people who still worshipped old pre-Christian gods. The Baltic crusades began in the early twelfth century and continued throughout the Middle Ages. In France, from 1209–1229, there was a crusade against **heretics** – people who followed a different version of Christianity. It was called the Albigensian Crusade after the town of Albi, a stronghold of the heretics. The war against the Muslims of Spain, lasting until 1492, was also declared to be a crusade.

Siege Warfare

FROM 1097 TO 1099, the army of the First **Crusade** moved slowly through Muslim territory, laying **siege** to castles and walled towns. The crusaders found that these were much more strongly built than any castles in Europe, and they had a hard time capturing them.

Siege Methods

There were four main methods of capturing a castle or walled town. The riskiest was an all-out attack, using ladders and siege towers (great wooden structures on wheels). The slowest way, which could take months, was to surround the place, to prevent supplies coming in, and starve the defenders into surrender. Attackers could also try to knock the walls down, by firing

This is a French picture of the siege of Antioch in 1098. Like all medieval art, this shows armour and buildings of the artist's own time, the fifteenth century.

Count Stephen of Blois described the siege of Antioch in a letter to his wife on 29 March 1098:

'We had frequent engagements with the Turks, seven battles in which we killed an innumerable quantity of them; they also killed many of our Christian brothers, sending their souls to the joys of heaven.

We found Antioch to be enormous beyond belief, and very strong and well-fortified. More than five thousand bold Turkish soldiers had flocked together within the city. Throughout the whole winter before Antioch we suffered bitter cold and driving rain for Christ our Lord.'

The capture of Jerusalem, from a fifteenth-century French manuscript. This was seen as the greatest Christian victory of the Middle Ages.

rocks from catapults, or digging tunnels beneath the walls and setting fires in them. The safest method was to try to get one of the defenders to betray his comrades and open the gates.

It took almost nine months for the crusaders to capture Antioch in the south of present-day Turkey, a city defended by 400 towers and so vast that it could not be surrounded. The crusaders camped before its walls and fought a series of **pitched battles** with the Turkish defenders. The Turks, who wore much lighter armour than the crusaders, were usually beaten. They rode ponies, and were armed with small bows and arrows, which could not penetrate the crusaders' heavy coats of **mail**. At the end of a battle, knights often had so many arrows sticking to them that they looked like hedgehogs.

Antioch was only finally captured, in June 1098, thanks to treachery. The commander of one of the towers agreed to open his gate to the crusaders in exchange for a large amount of silver.

Capturing Jerusalem

In June 1099, after almost three years on campaign, the crusaders laid siege to Jerusalem. On 15 July, they managed to break through the defences, and force their way into the city. Once inside they massacred all the Muslims they could find. Many Jews were also killed, for they too were believed to be the enemies of God.

A French crusader in the early twelfth century described the capture of Jerusalem:

'Our army overran the whole city, seizing gold and silver ... and houses full of riches of all kinds. All our men came rejoicing and weeping for joy, to worship at the church of the Holy Sepulchre ... Nearly the whole city was crammed with bodies. The Saracens [Arabs] who were still alive dragged the dead ones out in front of the gates, and made huge piles of them, as big as houses.'

Gesta Francorum (Deeds of the Franks).

17

Warrior Monks of Outremer

THE FIRST CRUSADE (1096–1099) set up four states in the Middle East: Jerusalem, Edessa, Antioch and Tripoli. Together, these were known in Europe as 'Outremer', a French word meaning 'overseas'. The new rulers, such as the king of Jerusalem and the count of Tripoli, tried to set up states like those they had left behind in Europe. They gave lands to lesser **nobles** in exchange for their military services. The problem was that there were not enough knights to make up an effective army. Perhaps no more than 2,000 knights had settled in the whole of Outremer.

Templars wore a white linen garment, called a 'surcoat' over their armour. It was often decorated with a red cross.

St Bernard of Clairvaux described a Templar as a new kind of warrior, living a religious life through war:

'The knight of Christ may strike with confidence and die even more confidently, for he serves Christ when he strikes, and serves himself when he falls ... If he kills an evildoer, he is not a mankiller, but ... a killer of evil ... Should he be killed himself, we know that he has not lost his life, but has come safely into port.'

In Praise of The New Knighthood,
St Bernard of Clairvaux, *circa* 1135.

Knights of the Temple

The problem of defending Outremer was partly solved by the setting up of new **military orders**. In 1119, a small group of knights in Jerusalem decided to form a **brotherhood** to protect pilgrims who were coming to visit the holy places. The king of Jerusalem gave them quarters on the site of the ancient Jewish temple. As a result, they became known as the Knights of the Temple of Solomon, or the Templars.

Templars were **warrior** monks. Like monks, they promised to live in poverty, and always to obey their superiors. Yet instead of withdrawing from the world and devoting their lives to religious worship, as monks did, members of the order could continue to follow the life of warfare that they had been trained for. Going on a crusade was meant to be only a temporary activity, a way of making amends for sins. This idea that a life of warfare could be holy was completely new in Christian thought.

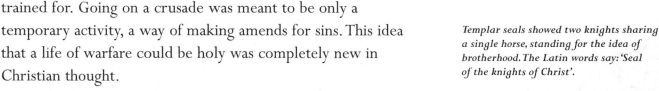

Templar seals showed two knights sharing a single horse, standing for the idea of brotherhood. The Latin words say: 'Seal of the knights of Christ'.

New Orders

Soon other orders were set up. There were the Hospitallers of St John, named after their lodging house for pilgrims in Jerusalem. German knights had their own brotherhood, the Order of Teutonic Knights. The strangest brotherhood was made up of knights suffering from leprosy, a terrible disease of the skin and nerves. It was named the Order of St Lazarus, after the **patron saint** of lepers.

The orders had their own houses, called preceptories, all over Europe. These were bases for recruiting new members, and for raising money for the defence of Outremer. Through gifts and grants of land, the orders became very wealthy.

Templar Banks

The Templars created Europe's first banking system. They invented a system of 'travellers' cheques'; pilgrims setting off from Europe could leave money at a Templar preceptory at home, and then withdraw the same sum when they reached Outremer. The Templars also lent large sums to kings, such as Louis VII of France (1137–1180), to help them pay for crusades.

Muslim Holy War

THE FIRST CRUSADE succeeded because the Muslims of the Middle East were divided. The rulers were so busy quarrelling with each other that they did not notice the threat from the crusaders until it was too late. However, in the twelfth century, a series of strong Muslim leaders appeared, who united their people and launched their own holy war, called a **jihad**, against Outremer. Just like the crusaders, Muslim holy warriors believed that they were fighting for God, and would be rewarded in heaven if they died in battle.

Saladin

The most famous of the Muslim leaders was Salah al-Din, known to Europeans as Saladin. He was a Kurd, born in northern Iraq. After seizing power in Egypt in 1169, he created a united Muslim empire and set about the conquest of the crusader states.

In 1187, Saladin led an army of 30,000 **warriors** against Tiberias, a town in the north of the kingdom of Jerusalem. To meet the threat, King Guy of Jerusalem (1186–1192) summoned an army of 20,000 men, the greatest crusader force ever assembled in Outremer. In early July, at the hottest time of the year, they marched across a waterless

The English friar, Roger Bacon, (*circa* 1220–1292) wrote an attack on crusading:

'War is not effective against unbelievers since the Church is sometimes defeated in crusades. Nor are unbelievers converted in this way but killed and sent to hell. Those who survive ... are more and more embittered against the Christian faith because of this violence.'

The Great Work, 1268.

Saladin's holy warriors ride to battle, in a fourteenth-century French painting.

plain towards Tiberias. On the evening of 4 July, they camped on two hills known as the Horns of Hattin. Saladin surrounded the camp, and his men set fire to the dry grass, irritating the thirsty crusaders with smoke.

The next morning, the Muslims launched their attack, crying 'God is great!' The knights, weakened by heat and thirst, fought bravely, but were overwhelmed. Guy surrendered to Saladin. In October, Saladin besieged and captured Jerusalem. When news of this reached Pope Urban III, he died of shock.

Later Crusades

Although some later crusades had limited successes, Jerusalem remained in Muslim hands. Churchmen were baffled that God had allowed his supposed enemies to be victorious. The only possible explanation was that the crusaders were being punished for their sins. Faced by repeated crusading failures, some churchmen went even further, and began to question the very idea of holy war.

Saint Louis

In 1248–54 and 1267–70, King Louis IX of France (1226–1270) led two crusades which both failed disastrously. His first expedition ended when he was captured with his whole army, and forced to pay a vast **ransom**. On his second attempt, he died of fever along with half his men. Louis had led such a holy life that he was declared to be a saint. So the failure of Louis' crusades could not be blamed on his sinfulness.

In this sixteenth-century Turkish painting, Muslim holy warriors drive the crusaders out of Jerusalem. Lying on the right are dead Christians, chopped into pieces.

Chivalry

BETWEEN THE ELEVENTH and the fourteenth centuries, the **warriors'** code of values grew more complicated. In the courts of southern France, a set of rules was developed, governing a knight's behaviour both on and off the battlefield. This code came to be called chivalry, from *chevalier*, the French word for 'knight'.

The central values of chivalry remained the old warrior ones of bravery, loyalty and generosity. There was also a new value, courtesy, or polite and respectful behaviour. Knights were now expected to be able to speak well, dance and write poetry, as well as fight.

Jousting – fighting single combats on horseback – was one way in which knights sought to impress their ladies.

The French court poet and historian, Jean Froissart described a typical fourteenth-century noble:

'Sir Eustace performed many fine feats of arms and no one could stand up to him, for he was young and deeply in love and full of enterprise ... [His lady] sent him love-letters and other tokens of great affection, by which the knight was inspired to still greater feats of bravery and accomplished such deeds that everyone talked of him.'

Chronicles, Jean Froissart, written between 1369–1400.

A knight receives a ring from a lady, a 'token' that he will wear in a tournament to show his devotion to her.

Noblewomen had high status in the southern French courts. Under their influence, chivalry gave a new importance to love. The perfect knight was one who was devoted to a lady. He would wear her 'token', such as a glove, when going into battle or fighting in a tournament. Love was believed to make a knight braver, for he would strive to be worthy of his lady.

Honour and Dishonour

According to chivalry, certain methods of fighting were honourable while others were dishonourable. The honourable way to fight was to send a challenge to the enemy, which was carried by a herald, or messenger. In battle, it was more honourable to fight face-to-face than to organize surprise attacks. If a knight surrendered and asked for quarter (mercy), his life would be spared and he would be well-treated. He would then pay his captor a **ransom**, a large sum of money in exhange for his freedom.

This chivalric code only applied to **nobles**. European knights had more in common with each other than with the common footsoldiers who served under them. Knights who spared their fellow knights in battle felt no shame in massacring footsoldiers and peasants. In real battles, knights often failed to live up to their chivalric code. Yet chivalry was of great importance to them. It helped them feel that they were superior to all other groups in medieval society. The shortcomings of knights led many writers to argue that standards were falling. They imagined that, at some time in the past, knights had lived according to their code. Even as early as the 1170s, a court poet called Chrétien de Troyes was complaining, 'The age of Chivalry is dead.'

The French poet Girault de Borneil criticized the failure of knights to live up to chivalry:

'Now only those who pillage or rob sheep are prized. Shame on the knight who protests his courtly love fresh from a raid on bleating lambs, or with stolen money from churches or pilgrims in his pocket.'

A poem from *circa* 1200, quoted in *Chivalry*, Michael Foss.

23

The Dead of Visby

IT IS HARD FOR US TODAY to imagine what it would have been like to take part in a medieval battle. Accounts written at the time, influenced by chivalric ideas, often make battles seem heroic, or give us only the bare facts and the numbers of the dead. It is only thanks to archaeology that we can begin to understand what it really meant to fight, and to die, on a medieval battlefield.

Mass Graves

In the summer of 1361, King Waldemar Atterdag of Denmark (1340–1375) invaded the Swedish island of Gotland with a large army of well-armed professional soldiers. On 27 July, the Danes and Gotlanders fought a great battle outside the town of Visby. The Gotlanders, mostly untrained and poorly armed peasants, were crushingly defeated.

After the battle, the dead were hurriedly buried outside the town walls in five mass graves. In the 1920s, archaeologists uncovered three of these graves, and found the bones of 1,185 men, some still wearing their armour.

This inscription was carved on a cross outside Visby:

'In the year of our Lord 1361, three days after St James's day, the Gotlanders fell before the gates of Visby into the hands of the Danes. Here lie they buried. Pray for them.'

The mass graves at Visby held gruesome discoveries for the archaeologists who dug into them.

Right: The bodies at Visby wore outdated armour, such as a type called 'lamellar', made from metal strips sown onto leather.

Below: The skull of one of the men killed at Visby, still wearing his mail hood.

Wounds

The bones showed several types of wound, each made by a different weapon. More than a hundred skulls had holes pierced by **crossbow** bolts, some several times. The Gotlanders must have come under a heavy crossbow attack at the start of the battle, before the armies were close enough for hand-to-hand fighting. The commonest wounds, 456 in all, were made by slashing weapons – swords and **battleaxes**. Most were found on the left side of the bodies, particularly the head. Such wounds would have been made by right-handed men using swinging blows. A sword or axe blow to the head was the quickest way to kill an enemy.

Another common slashing wound was to the legs. One man had both his upper legs sliced through with a single powerful blow. These leg wounds would not kill immediately, but would disable an enemy, who could be finished off later. Some of the skulls had large holes where they had been crushed, by **maces** and **war hammers**. Others had several small holes pierced by a 'morning star' – a wooden ball studded with spikes, swung on a chain. These weapons were often used to finish off people already lying on the ground. Many bodies showed several wounds, far more than were necessary to kill. This 'over-kill' suggests that the battle ended in a massacre, with the Danes hacking frenziedly at the helpless Gotlanders.

The Defenders

The ages of the dead of Visby ranged from sixteen to sixty, with some of the older men showing signs of severe arthritis (a disease that causes painful swollen joints). It seems that every male able to hold a weapon had been sent to fight the Danes.

Although many of the dead wore armour, it was out of date, and none of the bodies had a complete set. It is likely that all the available armour was shared out before the battle to as many people as possible.

The Hundred Years War

THE HUNDRED YEARS WAR is a name given to a conflict between England and France that lasted, on and off, from 1337 until 1453. The fighting was begun by King Edward III of England (1327–1377), who was the son of a French princess. In 1328, Edward's uncle, King Charles IV of France (1322–1328) died, leaving no son to succeed him. Charles was the last king from the Capetian **dynasty**, which had ruled France for 341 years.

As the closest male relative of the dead king, Edward believed that the French throne belonged to him. Yet the leading French nobles did not want a foreigner to rule over them, especially one who was only sixteen years old. They crowned Charles IV's cousin, Philip of Valois (Philip VI, 1328–1350), who founded a new royal dynasty.

Edward was the duke of Gascony, in southwest France, as well as king of England. Philip resented English rule in Gascony and, in 1337, he announced that Edward was no longer duke. Edward, now aged twenty-five, proclaimed that he was the true king of France, and prepared for war.

To show his claim to France, Edward III took to wearing the French royal coat of arms, yellow lilies, alongside his own royal emblem of three lions.

The Costs of War

France was the richest country in Europe, and had a population of twenty-one million people. England, with fewer than five million people, was a small and poor land in comparison. In order to pay for his war, Edward had to borrow vast sums of money from Italian and German bankers. He even **pawned** his gold crown.

Sea Battle

The first important battle of the war took place at sea, off the Flemish port of Sluys. In 1340, Edward learned that Philip had gathered a great fleet here and was planning to invade England.

Edward sailed from England in command of 260 ships, carrying 4,000 **men-at-arms** and 12,000 archers. On 24 June, he came upon the French, whose ships numbered between 300 and 500. The French ships, closely packed together, were so many that their masts were said to resemble a great forest.

There were two types of warship in each fleet. Most were sailing ships, high, slow vessels, with built-up turrets, called castles, at the back and front. These castles were fighting platforms for **archers** and crossbowmen. Alongside them were galleys, low, fast ships powered by dozens of oarsmen.

Like all medieval sea battles, Sluys was fought much like a battle on land. It began as soon as the fleets came in range of each other, with a **bombardment** of arrows and **crossbow** bolts. The ships then drew together so that the men-at-arms could engage in fierce hand-to-hand fighting.

The French historian, Jean Froissart described the fighting at Sluys:

'In order to come to closer quarters, they had great iron grappling hooks fixed to chains, and these they hurled into each other's ships to draw them together and hold them fast while the men engaged. Many deadly blows were struck and gallant deeds performed, ships and men were battered, captured and recaptured.'

Chronicles, Jean Froissart, 1369–1400.

This illustration from Froissart's history shows fierce hand-to-hand fighting, from ship to ship, at the Battle of Sluys. Many knights drowned, dragged under the water by the weight of armour.

English Victory

THE BATTLE OF SLUYS was a great victory for the English. It was said that if the fish could speak, they would have spoken French, because they had eaten so many drowned Frenchmen. The English captured almost two hundred enemy ships. No ships were sunk, for the aim of medieval naval warfare was always to capture ships rather than sink them. Sinking ships would have been seen as a terrible waste.

After losing his fleet, King Philip (1328–1350) could no longer threaten England with an invasion. As a result, all the battles of the Hundred Years War would be fought on French rather than English soil.

Victory Weapon

The reason for the victory was that the English possessed a deadly new tactic, or way of fighting, which the French had never seen before. This was a massed attack by hundreds of **archers** armed with **longbows**, so called because they were as tall as the men who fired them. A longbow's size gave it great range and power. It could kill at 36 metres, about the same range as a **crossbow**. Yet a crossbow could fire only three times a minute. In the same time, a longbowman could shoot twelve arrows. Longbows had been known for thousands of years, yet the English were the first people to use them as the main weapon in a battle.

English longbowmen can be seen in the foreground of this picture of Edward's capture of Caen in Normandy, in 1346.

Jean Froissart described Edward's victory celebrations after Sluys:

'After winning this victory, the English king spent the whole of the night...on board his ships at sea, amid such a banging and blowing of cymbals and trumpets, drums and cornets, that God's own thunder would not have been heard over it.'

Chronicles, Jean Froissart, 1369–1400.

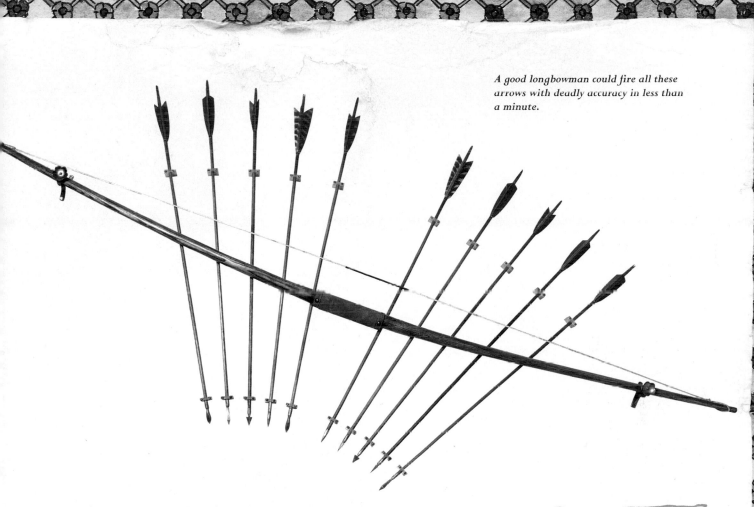

A good longbowman could fire all these arrows with deadly accuracy in less than a minute.

Longbows were made of yew, a strong but very springy wood. They were carved from the centre of the trunk, where soft sapwood lies beside harder heartwood. Each wood has different qualities, giving the bow its strength and power: the back of the bow was made from the sapwood, which resists stretching, while the belly, or underside, was made from heartwood, which resists compression (being pressed). This means that after the bow has been bent by the archer, it springs back to its original shape, sending the arrow flying.

It took great strength and skill to draw a longbow string and shoot the weapon accurately and rapidly. Longbowmen needed regular practice. Every Sunday, on village greens all over England, men shot at white cloth targets. In order to encourage longbow practice, one of King Edward's first acts at the start of his war was to ban all sports but archery on pain of death. Thanks to this weapon, the English were able to overwhelm the French at Sluys during the initial attack, raining many thousands of arrows onto the dismayed crews of the French ships.

Archers' Muscles

Repeated longbow practice since youth gave archers huge muscles in their wrists, right arms, shoulders and back. This resulted in thickening of the bones where the muscles were attached. Two skeletons found on the *Mary Rose*, a warship wrecked in 1545, were identified as longbowmen from this bone thickening. The skeletons also had misshapen backbones, probably caused by the pressure of drawing the bow while the body was twisted to one side.

The Campaign of Crécy

IN JULY 1346, Edward III (1327–1377) invaded Normandy with an army of 12–16,000 men, over half of them longbowmen. Edward led his army on a *chevauchée*, a 'horse ride' or plundering raid. His aim was to collect **booty** to pay his troops, and to bring shame on King Philip (1328–1350), whose duty it was to protect his French subjects.

The English marched east, burning towns and villages, until they reached the outskirts of the French capital, Paris, where Edward burned down the king's palace. This was a terrible humiliation for Philip. Edward then headed north, until he reached a village called Crécy, where he decided to make a stand.

Battle of Crécy

Seeking revenge, King Philip rode north to Crécy at the head of an army which was triple the size of Edward's, and included 12,000 mounted knights and 6,000 crossbowmen, **mercenaries** from Genoa in Italy. Knowing he would be outnumbered, Edward prepared a strong defensive position on the

This picture of Crécy shows the victory of English longbowmen, on the right, over the French king's crossbowmen, who lie dead and dying.

This chivalric view of Crécy, which shows the rival kings in hand-to-hand fighting, ignores the longbowmen who really won the battle.

brow of a hill. He ordered his knights and other **men-at-arms** to dismount and send their horses to the rear. They stood beside the massed **archers**, waiting for the French to attack.

On the afternoon of 26 August, the French came within sight of the English. Philip wanted to wait until the following day to fight, for his men were tired after marching since daybreak. However, the undisciplined French knights disobeyed his orders, for none of them wanted to be the first to halt. They continued riding towards the English position until battle was unavoidable.

Forced to fight, at 4pm, Philip sent his Genoese crossbowmen against the English. They advanced up the hill, giving loud war cries to encourage themselves. When they believed that they were within range, they fired their **crossbows**. With the low sun in their eyes, they misjudged the distance, and their bolts all fell short. Before the Genoese had time to reload, the English longbowmen were firing tens of thousands of arrows down on them. The Genoese retreated, running into the French knights who were now charging towards the English.

The French were soon in confusion. Philip sent wave after wave of knights into the battle. His **cavalry** made more than a dozen mass charges, but each time fell before the arrows of the longbowmen. By nightfall, many of France's leading **nobles** lay dead, including a duke, six counts and two thousand knights. Philip himself had been wounded in the neck and thigh, and had had two horses killed under him.

Blind Bravery

Among those killed at Crécy was Philip's brother-in-law, King John of Bohemia (1311–1346). Although fifty-one years old and blind, John had asked to be pointed at the enemy so that he could strike just one blow. Some knights tied their horses' reins to the king's and led him towards the English. The next day, all were found dead, their horses still tied together.

The Black Prince's War

TEN YEARS AFTER THEIR VICTORY at Crécy, the English invaded France again. Now they were led by the king's son, Edward Prince of Wales, who had fought at Crécy as a sixteen year old. Edward is better known as the 'Black Prince', a nickname given to him by the French, perhaps from the colour of his armour. The prince's opponent was the new French king, John II (1350–1364), nicknamed 'the Good'.

Battle of Poitiers

The campaign began with a plundering raid of western France, starting from English territory in Gascony. King John pursued the English, who were laden down with **booty** and moving slowly, to the town of Poitiers, where he cut off their line of retreat back to Gascony. The Black Prince would be forced to face an army twice the size of his own.

On 19 September 1356, the Black Prince drew up his army on a wooded slope near Poitiers. He had a long hedge in front of him, pierced by a road, where he positioned his **archers**.

This fifteenth-century painting shows King John, in gold armour, surrendering to the Black Prince at the Battle of Poitiers.

New Armour

By the middle of the fourteenth century, **mail** had given way to **steel plate armour**, with glancing surfaces, offering much greater protection from arrows and crossbow bolts. Shields, no longer as important, grew smaller or were abandoned altogether, allowing knights to use both arms to fight with long swords and **maces**. Fighting, now often on foot, demanded great fitness.

King John believed that the English had won at Crécy because their knights fought as footsoldiers. So he ordered most of his knights to dismount, and to attack the English on foot. John did not realize that it would be much easier for the English knights, fighting a defensive battle on foot, than for the French, who would have to rush up a hillside wearing heavy armour. He also threw away his advantage in numbers by making his knights attack on a narrow front, sending them in a wedge towards the gap in the hedge. This meant that the French knights would be crowded together, allowing the longbowmen to concentrate their fire on them.

The result was another disaster for the French. Many knights were killed by arrows, which could pierce armour at close range. Those who broke through the archers were so exhausted that the English **men-at-arms** easily defeated them. At the end, King John was captured along with his son and seventeen counts.

Jean Froissart described the Black Prince's treatment of his noble prisoners after the battle:

'The Prince of Wales gave a supper for the king of France and most of the captured counts and barons ... He himself served in all humility both at the king's table and at the others, steadfastly refusing to sit down with the king, in spite of all his entreaties. He insisted that he was not yet worthy to sit at the table of so mighty a prince and so brave a soldier as he had proved himself to be on that day.'

Chronicles, Jean Froissart, 1369–1400.

The tomb of the Black Prince in Canterbury is topped with this effigy of him, praying and wearing full armour.

Chivalry in Decline

THE BLACK PRINCE wanted to be seen as a defender of the code of chivalry, as his treatment of his royal prisoner, King John (1350–1364), shows. Yet his victories undermined that code, for they showed that humble **archers** were the equal of knights on the battlefield. The French knights, who had tried to fight according to their old ideas of honourable warfare, had been killed in their thousands.

'Hog in Armour'

It was only when the French abandoned chivalric warfare that they were able to find a way to fight effectively against the English. The man who came up with the new tactics was Bertrand du Guesclin (1320–1380), who belonged to a poor yet **noble** family from Brittany. He was small, stout and so ugly that he was described as a 'hog in armour'. Yet he was one of the few French knights who understood military leadership. From 1370–80, he served the new king, Charles V (1364–1380), as his constable, or chief military commander.

Routiers

Du Guesclin's soldiers were not knights but **mercenaries**, mostly from the lower classes. They were known as *'routiers'* (highwaymen), 'scorchers' and 'skinners', from their lawless and violent behaviour. When they were not fighting the English, they often lived by plundering French towns and villages. Aimerigot Marcel, a *routier* captain, later boasted, 'We were fed like kings, and when we rode forth the country trembled before us.'

After his death in 1380, Bertrand du Guesclin was honoured with a fine tomb in the Church of St Denis, the burial place of France's kings and queens.

Henry V of England, on the left, invades France in 1415. Although this picture shows two mounted longbowmen, it was very difficult to fire a longbow while riding a horse.

Du Guesclin avoided fighting **pitched battles** with the English.
This was easy to do, because English tactics depended on taking up a strong defensive position and waiting for the French to attack. Instead, he specialized in ambushes, night attacks, and hit-and-run raids. The aim was to wear down the invading armies little by little and gradually win back captured territory. Today, we call du Guesclin's methods '**guerrilla** warfare', from a Spanish word meaning 'little war'.

By the time of du Guesclin's death, in 1380, the English had lost most of their earlier gains. In 1389, both sides, exhausted by the war, agreed to a temporary peace.

Chivalry Revived

War broke out again in 1415, when King Henry V of England (1413–1422) invaded France with a tiny army of just 6,000 men, 5,000 of them archers. The defeats at Crécy and Poitiers were now just a distant memory, and the French knights revived their chivalric tactics, with disastrous results.

At Agincourt, on 25 October 1415, Henry's men took up a defensive position between two woods, and stuck sharpened stakes in the ground in front of them. The French knights made frontal charges, on horseback and on foot, across the narrow battlefield, which had turned into a squishy bog after heavy rain. Some 6,000 of them were killed, and Agincourt would be remembered as the greatest English victory of the Hundred Years War. The French knights' use of outdated tactics shows just how deeply ingrained their ideas of chivalry were.

A French nobleman described the battle of Agincourt:

'**Numbers of the French were slain and severely wounded by the English bowmen ... The horses were become unmanageable, so that horses and riders were tumbling on the ground, and the whole army was thrown into disorder ... The English took instant advantage of the disorder ... and, throwing down their bows, fought lustily with swords, hatchets, mallets, and bill-hooks, slaying all before them.'**

Chronicles, Enguerrand de Monstrelet, *circa* 1440s.

Joan of Arc

FOLLOWING HIS VICTORY at Agincourt, Henry V (1413–1422) conquered Normandy, and formed an alliance with the powerful duke of Burgundy in south-east France. In 1420, the English and Burgundians forced the mentally ill French king, Charles VI (1380–1422), to disown his son, the **dauphin** (prince) Charles, and agree to make Henry his heir.

In 1422, both Henry and King Charles died. The dauphin claimed the throne, though he could find few supporters. He was a weak man whose confidence had been greatly shaken when his father disowned him. His troops were beaten again and again by the English, now fighting in the name of Henry V's baby son, Henry VI (1422–1461).

Girl Commander

Joan of Arc was a farmer's daughter, born in about 1412. At the age of thirteen, Joan believed that she was hearing voices. The voices identified themselves as Saint

Joan wears gold armour and rides a great white war horse in this picture, from a French book of 1505.

Joan dictated a letter to the English, which was fired from a crossbow into an English-held fort at Orleans:

'You, men of England, who have no right to be in this kingdom of France, the King of Heaven entreats and orders you through me, Joan the Maiden, to abandon your forts and go back to your own country; or I will make such a disturbance as will be eternally remembered.'

Joan of Arc's third letter to the English at Orléans, 5 May, 1429.

Catherine, Saint Margaret and Saint Michael. At first the saints gave her simple messages, telling her to be good and to go to church. Then they said that she had been chosen to drive the English out of France. To start with, Joan tried to ignore these voices, but their message did not change.

Showing great determination, in February 1429, Joan found her way to the dauphin's court at Pontheiu. She convinced Charles and his leading churchmen that her voices were genuine. The dauphin gave her a suit of armour, a banner, and the rank of military commander. Joan, who was just seventeen, knew nothing about warfare. She would be a figurehead for the soldiers, while experts made the important military decisions.

Joan's self-belief impressed everybody who met her. Word spread among the French troops that they had a saint at their head, and their morale, or fighting spirit, grew. In May 1429, Joan led her army against the English, who had been besieging the city of Orléans for eight months. In a little over a week, the siege was lifted. Joan then marched on Reims, deep within enemy territory, where French kings were traditionally crowned. On 17 July, in Reims, Joan watched the dauphin become King Charles VII (1422–1461).

A nineteenth-century image shows the dauphin being crowned while Joan gazes up to heaven. The light streaming from above is meant to show God's approval of the coronation.

Burned at the Stake

Joan of Arc's military career was a short one. In May 1430, she was captured by the Burgundians, who handed her over to their English allies. The English said that Joan's voices were those of devils, not saints. Found guilty of witchcraft and heresy, on 30 May 1431, she was burned to death in the marketplace of Rouen.

Gunpowder

THE ENGLISH FINALLY LOST the Hundred Years War because of a new weapon, which would change the way that wars were fought for ever: gunpowder. Its recipe, made by mixing sulphur, charcoal and a white salty substance called saltpetre, was invented by the Chinese, who first described it in the eleventh century. The recipe was known in Europe by 1300 and, soon after, small cannon were being made, at first in Italy.

Bombards

Simple cannon were used at Crécy and Agincourt, though they could do little except make a lot of noise and smoke. In time, cannon grew larger and more powerful. By the middle of the fifteenth century, there was no castle wall that could stand up to them. **Sieges**, which once dragged out for months, would now be over in a matter of days. Between May 1449 and August 1450, the French used cannon to retake more than seventy English strongholds.

Meanwhile the Turks were using enormous cannon to attack the **Byzantine Empire**. In 1453, the walls of the Byzantine capital, Constantinople, which were the

Cannon were felt to have their own personalities. They were often given names, with verses inscribed on their barrels:

**'I am Dragon the poisonous serpent
Who desires with furious blows
To drive off our enemies.
Jehan le Noir, master gunmaker
Conrad, Coin and Cradinteur
All master founders
Made me on time in 1476.'**

War in the Middle Ages, Philippe Contamine.

In this painting, small early cannon are used in a siege alongside other weapons, such as longbows.

This castle at Assissi in Italy has a low tower on the left, with thick sloping walls. It is typical of towers built to withstand cannon.

strongest in Europe, were battered down by Turkish cannon. Constantinople became a Turkish city, which is today called Istanbul.

These first great cannon, called **bombards**, fired stone balls. They were mounted on fixed platforms, and could only be used in sieges. In the 1450s, the French began to make iron cannon balls. Iron is heavier than stone, and so small iron balls could cause as much damage as large stone ones. This meant that cannon did not have to be so huge. From the 1490s, they were mounted on wheels and pulled by horses into battle.

Effects of the Cannon

As a result of the use of cannon, fortifications had to change. In the 1460s, high castle walls began to be replaced by low, thick ones, with heavy earth embankments to absorb the impact of cannon balls. Circular towers were replaced with angled ones, exposing a smaller area to **bombardment**. The towers had wide, flat tops, and now could be used as gun platforms. These new lower walls were vulnerable to **infantry** attack, so deep outer ditches were also dug, to keep the enemy at a distance.

Cannon also changed warfare at sea, for it was now easy for warships to sink each other. Instead of coming close for hand-to-hand fighting, as the English and French fleets did at Sluys in 1340 (see pages 27–28), warships began to fight from a distance, exchanging 'broadsides', cannon bombardments aimed at each other's hulls (body of a ship).

Killed by his own Cannon

Early cannon could be as dangerous to their owners as to the enemy. In 1460, King James II of Scotland (1437–1460) was besieging Roxburgh castle in southern Scotland, held by the English. James, who was fascinated by cannon, was curious to see a new great bombard, called 'the Lion', fired. When the bombard was fired, it blew into bits, tearing James's leg off. The king quickly bled to death. James was the first ruler of any country to be killed by gunfire.

Marching to War

WHILE THE FRENCH KNIGHTS were falling under the arrows of English longbowmen, half way across Europe another people, the Swiss, found their own way to defeat knights on horseback. Like gunpowder, the Swiss methods would eventually change the way that European wars were fought.

Mountains and Lakes

Switzerland is a mountainous country, with lakes, forests and isolated valleys. Partly as a result of this landscape, the Swiss did not belong to a single state. Instead, they lived in small self-governing communities, called cantons. Surrounded by powerful neighbours, the cantons joined together for mutual protection, forming a loose grouping called a confederation. In wartime, each canton supplied soldiers to the army of the confederation. These soldiers were **militiamen** who owned their own weapons, and trained together in their spare time.

Pikemen and Halbardiers

Swiss footsoldiers used two weapons – the pike, or long thrusting spear, and the halberd, a pole tipped with a point, with a **hatchet** blade on one side and a spike on the other. The halberd could be jabbed like a spear, swung like a **battleaxe**, and used to hook riders off their horses or jerk their reins away.

Swiss pikemen march in a tight mass across a battlefield. On the right another group of Swiss use the cover of a wood to mount a bloody ambush.

Pikemen wore simple helmets, like this Spanish example, sometimes combined with armour protecting the face and neck.

Swiss pikemen and halbardiers would advance in a tight mass, shoulder to shoulder. To fight like this, the men had to learn to move as a single group, marching in step to the beat of a drum. The success of this tactic was first shown in 1339 at the Battle of Laupen. At Laupen, a Swiss army of footsoldiers defeated a much larger force of mounted Burgundian knights on an open plain, where the horsemen would have been expected to win.

The Swiss marched swiftly towards the Burgundians in three columns, and then formed 'hedgehogs', squares bristling on all sides with lowered pikes and halberds. After beating off a series of charges by the knights, the Swiss drove the Burgundians from the battlefield.

Victories such as Laupen increased the confidence of the Swiss, and made them the most feared soldiers in Europe. In part this was because of the contempt they showed for chivalry. They did not see the point of taking prisoners, preferring to kill all the defeated.

Landsknechte

Swiss methods were so successful that they were copied. In the 1480s, in southern Germany, soldiers calling themselves Landsknechte ('country companions') began to arm and train like the Swiss. Both the *Landsknechte* and the Swiss hired themselves out to foreign armies as **mercenaries**. As a result, in the sixteenth century, the beat of the drum would be heard on battlefields across the whole of Europe.

The Swiss had the reputation of the most fearless soldiers in Europe. The Italian writer Niccolo Machiavelli gave one reason for Swiss bravery:

'The Swiss ... never shun an engagement even if terrified by artillery. Instead, they punish with death those who break ranks or show any sign of fear ... The condemned are publicly put to death by the other soldiers.'

The Seven Books on the Art of War,
Niccolo Machiavelli, 1520.

A halberd, with its three deadly features – the pointed tip, the hatchet blade and the spike.

The Wars of the Roses

A CIVIL WAR is one fought between people of the same nation. In England, the year 1455 saw the beginning of a series of civil wars which lasted for over thirty years. These were fought by rival branches of the English royal family, known as the Yorkists and the Lancastrians. Their conflict is called the 'Wars of the Roses', a name invented much later, in the belief that the Lancastrians and the Yorkists chose different-coloured roses as their badges. In fact, the white rose was one of several Yorkist badges, while the Lancastrians only adopted a red rose at the very end of the wars.

The English king Henry VI (1422–1461), who belonged to the Lancastrian family, was a weak ruler, who suffered from bouts of madness when he was unable to speak or stand up. Real power in England lay with whoever could control the king. In the 1450s, there was a bitter quarrel between a group of nobles led by the queen, Margaret of Anjou, and another group, led by Richard, Duke of York. While the king was suffering from madness, York was able to rule the kingdom as '**protector**'. When Henry recovered, power passed back to the queen's party. Eventually

This Lancastrian picture shows Henry VI as a warrior king. He is encircled by the red rose of Lancaster.

Philippe de Commynes described England during the Wars of the Roses:

'The realm of England enjoys one favour above all other realms, that neither the countryside nor the people are destroyed nor are buildings burnt or demolished. Misfortune falls on soldiers and on nobles in particular.'

Memoirs, Philippe de Commynes, 1498.

this quarrel led to open warfare. At first, York was simply fighting in order to rule on behalf of the king. Then, in 1460, he laid claim to the crown itself.

When Richard of York was killed in battle, in 1461, his son Edward became the Yorkist leader. The same year, Edward won a great victory over the Lancastrians at Towton. Around 12,000 Yorkists and 20,000 Lancastrians died at Towton, making this the bloodiest battle ever fought in Britain. The victor was crowned Edward IV (1461–1483).

In 1470, it was the Lancastrians' turn to win a victory. Henry became king again, while Edward fled the country. The following year, Edward was back, defeating the Lancastrians and killing Henry VI.

The wars only finally ended in the 1480s. In 1485, Edward's brother, Richard III (1483–1485) was killed by Henry Tudor at the Battle of Bosworth. He became King Henry VII (1485–1509), founding a new royal dynasty, the Tudors. The last serious fighting took place in 1487 at the Battle of Stoke, where Henry crushed a Yorkist uprising.

Effects of the Wars

Although eighteen battles took place during the Wars of the Roses, the ordinary people of England were mostly left in peace. The leaders on each side wanted to rule a wealthy kingdom and to win the support of the people. So there were none of the raids which had caused so much suffering in France during the Hundred Years War. The people who suffered most were the nobility. At the end of each battle, the victors usually killed all the **nobles** they could capture. As a result, many of England's leading families were completely wiped out.

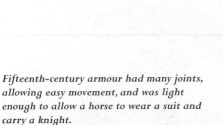

Fifteenth-century armour had many joints, allowing easy movement, and was light enough to allow a horse to wear a suit and carry a knight.

New Armies

FOR MOST OF THE MIDDLE AGES, armies were only recruited for a limited period in wartime. When they needed them, rulers summoned knights who owed them service, called up **militiamen**, or hired **mercenaries**.

In 1445–1446, King Charles VII of France (1483–1498), found a new way of raising troops. He set up the first standing, or full-time, army. It was made up of twenty companies, each comprising 600 horsemen. They were well-paid and based in **garrison** towns throughout France. Charles went on to employ full-time **archers** and Swiss pikemen. Now the French king had an army at his disposal whenever he needed it.

At the beginning of the Middle Ages, any small group of mounted **warriors** could take to warfare, and set off on raids. By the second half of the fifteenth century, this was no longer possible. The new standing armies, with their expensive cannon, could only be afforded by powerful rulers. Waging war had become a very expensive business.

In 1066, an army of 7,000 Normans had been enough for the conquest of England. Late-fifteenth century kings could not expect to win wars with such small forces. When Charles VIII of France invaded Italy in 1494, he led an army of 25,000 men.

At the Battle of Pavia, in 1525, around 3,000 French mounted men-at-arms were killed by Spaniards using deadly new handguns. Pavia has been called the first modern battle.

Science of War

Jean de Bueil, an old man who had fought in the Hundred Years War, was present at a council of war held by King Louis XI (1461–1483) in 1471. He said to the king, 'I am not accustomed to see so many troops together. How do you prevent disorder and confusion among such a mass?'

The answer was that the soldiers had to be highly disciplined. The Swiss methods of drilling to the beat of a drum were now widespread. Deserting, or running away, became a punishable offence. The commanders also needed a new professional approach to war. They had to understand how to use their **artillery**, their **cavalry** and their **infantry** in the proper ways. War had become a science, and many instruction manuals on warfare began to be written.

The chivalric idea that **nobles** were more valuable in battle than commoners was also forgotten. Armies gave up the practice of taking prisoners for **ransom**. This was a distraction from the main business, defeating the enemy. As a result, sixteenth-century battles would be even more ferocious than those of the Middle Ages.

The Arquebus

War was transformed by the arquebus, the first effective handgun, invented in Spain in the mid fifteenth century. It had a higher rate of fire than a **crossbow** while, unlike a **longbow**, demanding little training or skill. It was mostly used by footsoldiers, though there were also troops of mounted arquebusiers.

Above: An early arquebus.

Below: This late-fifteenth-century painting shows arquebusiers fighting alongside cannon, which have been wheeled onto the battlefield.

A French nobleman, Blaise de Monluc (1501–1571), described handguns as cowardly, unchivalrous weapons:

'**Would to God that this miserable device had never been invented. I would not then have received those wounds from which I now suffer; nor would so many brave man have been slain, mostly by pitiful wretches; mean-spirited cowards who would not have dared to look those men in the face, whom at a distance they laid dead with their confounded bullets. This was the devil's invention to make us murder each other.'**

Commentaries, Blaise de Monluc, 1570s.

Timeline

1002–13	Svein Forkbeard of Denmark raids England.
1027	Church Council at Elne in southern France tries to limit fighting to certain days (Monday to Wednesday).
1030	King Olaf the Good of Norway is killed at the Battle of Stiklestad.
1061	Normans invade Sicily.
1066	Norman conquest of England.
1095	Pope Urban II proclaims the First Crusade.
1099	Crusaders capture Jerusalem.
1119	Knights Templar are founded.
1187	Saladin captures Jerusalem.
1209–29	**Crusade** against heretics, called Cathars, in southern France.
1270	King Louis IX of France dies in Tunis while on crusade.
1291	Muslims capture Acre, last Christian stronghold in the Middle East.
1339	The Swiss defeat the Burgundians at the Battle of Laupen.
1337	Beginning of the Hundred Years War between France and England.
1340	English defeat French fleet at the Battle of Sluys.
1346	English longbowmen beat French knights at the Battle of Crécy.
1356	King John of France is captured by the Black Prince at the Battle of Poitiers.
1361	Danes massacre Gotlanders at the Battle of Visby.
1370–80	Bertrand du Guesclin uses '**guerrilla**' tactics against the English.
1386	Swiss defeat the Austrians at the Battle of Sempach.
1415	Henry V of England wins great victory over the French at Agincourt.
1429	Joan of Arc relieves Orleans, besieged by the English.
1445	King Charles VII of France sets up first standing army.
1455–87	Wars of the Roses in England.
1449–50	Using cannon, French retake most of the strongholds held by the English.
1450s	Iron cannon balls used by the French.
1453	Turks capture Constantinople.
1460	King James II of Scotland is killed when his cannon accidentally blows up.
1480s	German *Landsknechte* appear.
1492	Christians complete the 'reconquest' of Muslim Spain.
1494	King Charles VIII of France invades Italy, using cannon on wheels.

Further Information

Books to Read

DK Discoveries: Castle at War by Andrew Langley and Peter Dennis (Dorling Kindersley, 1998)

DK Eyewitness Guide: Castle by Christopher Gravett (Dorling Kindersley, 2000)

DK Eyewitness Guide: Knight by Christopher Gravett (Dorling Kindersley, 2000)

A Medieval Castle by Fiona McDonald and Mark Bergin (Peter Bedrick books, 1993)

The Wars of the Roses: A Concise History by Charles Ross (Thames and Hudson, 1986)

The World of the Medieval Knight by Christopher Gravett (Hodder Wayland, 2001)

Sources

Chivalry by Michael Foss (Book Club Associates, 1975)

Chronicles by Jean Froissart (Penguin Classics, 1968)

Chronicles of the Age of Chivalry edited by Elizabeth Hallam (Guild Publishing, 1989)

Chronicles of the Crusades edited by Elizabeth Hallam (Weidenfeld and Nicolson)

Commentaires by Blaise de Monluc (Gallimard, 1964)

Critics of the Crusade (N.V. Swets and Zeitlinger, 1940)

English Historical Documents edited by David C. Douglas (Eyre Methuen, 1981)

King Harald's Saga by Snorri Sturluson, translated by Magnus Magnusson and Hermann Palsson (Penguin Classics, 1966)

Memoirs by Philippe de Commynes, (Penguin Classics, 1972)

The Anglo-Saxon Chronicle translated and edited by G.N. Garmondsway (Everyman, 1953)

War in the Middle Ages by Philippe Contamine (Blackwell, 1984)

Glossary

anarchy The absence of rule in a state. The word, which is Greek, means 'no rule'. An example of anarchy would be a state where nobody obeys the laws.

archer Someone armed with a bow and arrows.

artillery Heavy firearms, such as cannon.

bailey A courtyard in a Norman castle.

battleaxe An axe with a long wooden handle and a large flat iron head with a sharp edge, used in battle.

bombard A large cannon used in siege warfare, from the fourteenth century.

bombardment Continual attack.

booty Goods or money seized by soldiers in warfare.

brotherhood A grouping of men who join together for a particular purpose. The Knights Templar, who joined together for the purpose of protecting pilgrims, called themselves a 'brotherhood'.

Byzantine Empire The Greek Empire, ruled from Constantinople (present-day Istanbul in Turkey). It lasted from the fourth century until 1453, when Constantinople was captured by the Turks.

cavalry Soldiers who fight on horseback.

crossbow A bow placed crosswise on a wooden stock, or handle. The string is pulled or winched back to a catch, which is released by a trigger, firing a short arrow, called a bolt.

crusade A Christian holy war. The name comes from 'croix', French for cross.

dauphin The French title of the prince who was the king's eldest son, and heir to the throne.

dynasty A family line of rulers.

fealty Loyalty, the duty owed by a vassal (see below) to his lord. The word is French and means 'faithful'.

garrison A military building, such as a fort, where troops are stationed.

granaries Large buildings where grain is stored.

guerrilla 'Little war', a method of fighting using small actions, such as hit-and-run raids, rather than battles.

hatchet A small axe, held in one hand.

heretic A Christian holding beliefs opposed by the Church.

housecarls Soldiers in the personal service of the king of England before 1066.

infantry Soldiers who fight on foot.

jihad A Muslim holy war. The word is Arabic and means 'struggle'.

lance A spear used by horsemen.

longbow A bow which is as tall as the archer who fires it. It is called a longbow to distinguish it from shorter bows and crossbows.

mace A club, with a long handle and a heavy metal head.

mail Armour made from hundreds of tiny metal rings.

men-at-arms Knights and commoners armed as knights (called sergeants).

mercenary A soldier who fights for pay, often for a foreign power.

military orders Brotherhoods of Christian holy warriors, such as the Knights Templar.

militiamen Part-time soldiers, fighting for their own city or country.

motte The mound of earth on which a Norman castle was built.

noble Someone believed to have special status as a result of being born into a particular powerful family. Nobles are said to be of 'high birth'.

non-combatants People who are not involved in fighting in time of war.

patron saint A saint in charge of a particular country, activity, or illness. For example, Saint Andrew is the patron saint of Scotland. In the Middle Ages, he was also believed to help cure sore throats.

pawned To offer something as a pledge for a loan.

penance Any action performed by a Christian, at the command of the Church, to make amends to God for a sin.

pilgrimage A journey to a holy place for religious reasons.

pitched battle A deliberate battle. In a pitched battle, unlike a siege, a raid, or a surprise attack, the commanders on each side willingly decide to fight, and choose where to place their forces.

protection money Money demanded by raiders as the price for being left unharmed. People who agreed to pay bought protection from attack.

protector A person who rules a kingdom in the place of a monarch.

ransom Money paid for the return of a captured warrior.

siege An attempt by an army to capture a fortified town or a castle. The attackers surrounded the castle or town, so that nobody could escape, and then launched an attack, or waited for the defenders to run out of supplies.

steel plate armour Armour made from steel plates, shaped to cover as much of the body as possible.

vassal Someone who swears to serve a powerful lord, usually in return for the right to hold land. The word originally meant 'servant'.

war hammer A hammer with a long wooden handle and a heavy iron head, used as a weapon.

warriors People who live by making war.

Index